Let's discuss

ENERGY RESOURCES

Solar Power

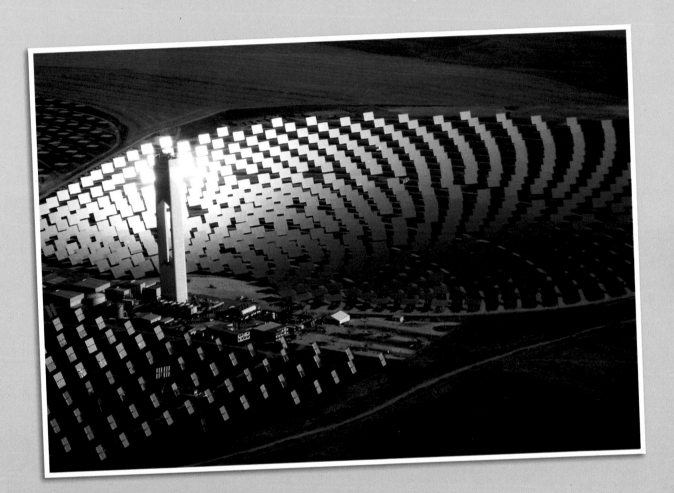

Richard and Louise Spilsbury

WAYLAND

First published in 2010 by Wayland

Copyright © Wayland 2010

Wayland
338 Euston Road
London NW1 3BH

Wayland Australia
Level 17/207 Kent Street
Sydney, NSW 2000

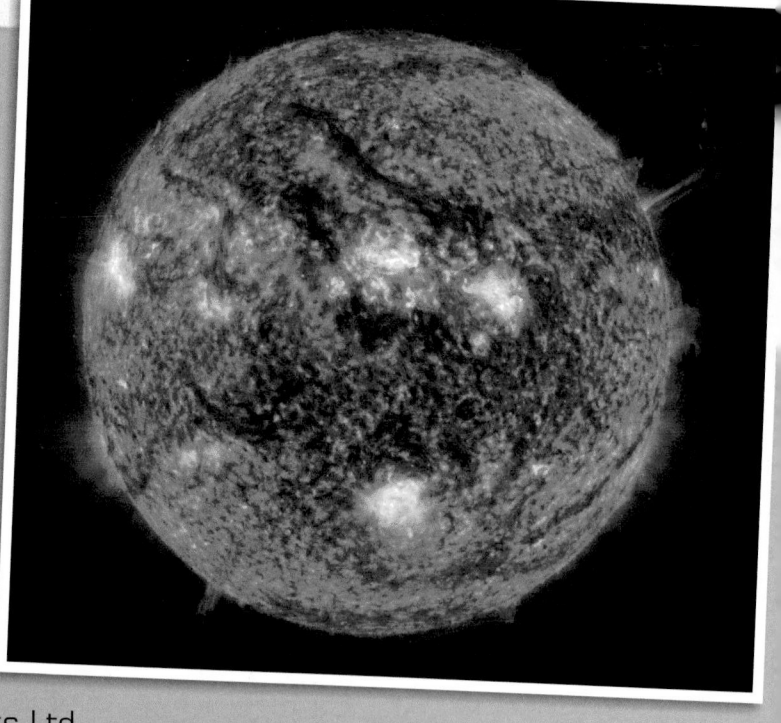

Editorial director: Rasha Elsaeed
Produced for Wayland by Discovery Books Ltd
Managing editor: Rachel Tisdale
Designer: Ian Winton
Illustrator: Stefan Chabluk
Picture researchers: Rachel Tisdale and Tom Humphrey

Picture credits: AORA: p. 9 (Haim Fried); Barefoot Photographers of Tilonia: p. 15 (Flickr); BP: p. 29 (Makai Construction); Construction Photography: p. 5; Coolearth Solar: p. 27; Corbis: p. 24 (Jim Young/Reuters); Desert Tec – UK (www.trec-uk.org.uk): p. 16 & title page (Sandia National Laboratories), p. 21 (Sandia National Laboratories); Flickr: p. 26 (Gnal); Getty Images: p. 18 (Kay Chernush/The Image Bank); Helios Resource: p. 22; NASA: p. 7 (ESA/SOHO), p. 14, p. 28 (Solar Impulse Company); NREL: p. 13 (Southern California Edison); Photolibrary: p. 10 (Maximilian Stock Ltd.); Shutterstock: cover (Pinosub), p. 6 (Otmar Smit), p. 11 (John Keith), p. 19 (Darren J Bradley), p. 20 (SphinxHK); SXC: p. 4 (www.sxc.hu).

British Library Cataloguing in Publication Data

Spilsbury, Richard, 1963-
   Solar power. – (Let's discuss energy resources)
   1. Solar energy–Juvenile literature.
   I. Title II. Series III. Spilsbury, Louise.
   333.7'923-dc22

ISBN: 978 0 7502 6152 4

Printed in China

Wayland is a division of Hachette Children's Books, an Hachette UK company.
www.hachette.co.uk

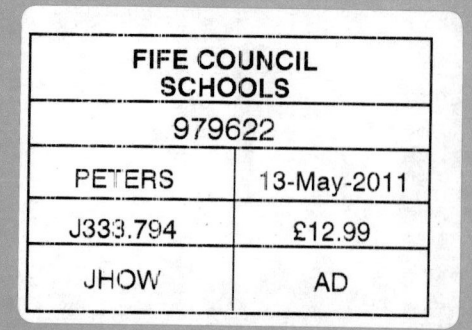

Contents

The words in **bold** can be found in the glossary on page 31.

Solar power as an energy resource

We use energy resources every day, without thinking about it! Cars burn fuel in engines to release the energy that turns their wheels. Sun shining through greenhouse windows warms the air to help plants grow. From mobile phones to DVD players, most of the machines we use run on electricity made using energy resources.

Energy resources

Most of the energy that we use to make electricity comes from **fossil fuels**, such as coal, oil and gas. These energy resources took millions of years to form underground from the buried remains of ancient plants and animals. Worldwide, about 67 per cent of electricity is made in fossil fuel **power stations**, mostly from coal. These power stations burn fossil fuels to make heat energy that can be used to make electricity.

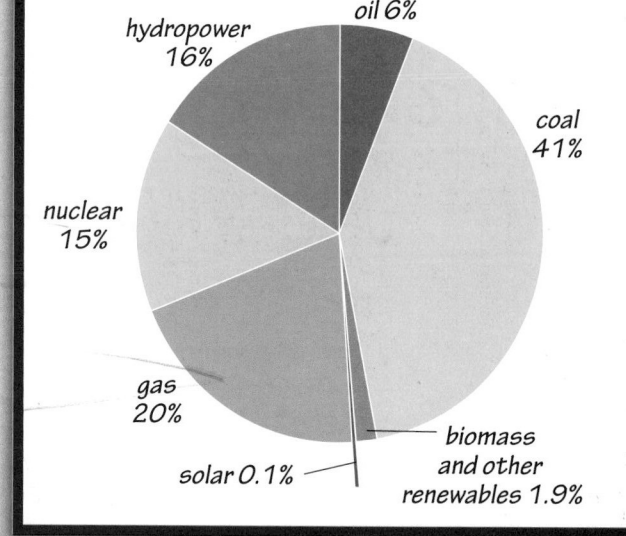

Global electricity from different energy resources

- hydropower 16%
- oil 6%
- coal 41%
- nuclear 15%
- gas 20%
- solar 0.1%
- biomass and other renewables 1.9%

Problems with fossil fuels

One problem with fossil fuels is that there is a limited amount in the Earth. Scientists think that coal, oil and gas could all run out within 200 years if we carry on using as much electricity, and fuel in our vehicles, as we do today. Another problem is that burning fossil fuels to release heat also releases gases into the **atmosphere**.

The major problem with using fossil fuels to generate electricity is the production of **greenhouse gases** that build up in the atmosphere.

Some of these gases cause **pollution**, which can harm people and the environment. Others, such as **carbon dioxide** gas, are types of greenhouse gases that build up and store heat from the Sun in the atmosphere. Most scientists believe this is causing **global warming**, which is rapidly changing weather patterns across the world. This climate change is causing flooding and droughts.

Renewable energy resources

Renewable energy resources will not run out because they are in endless supply. These resources include sunlight, wind, waves, tides and biomass. Biomass is renewable fuel made from plant and animal material, including wood, crops and manure and some household rubbish. Fossil fuels are **non-renewable** because they are not forming naturally as people use them up. Using renewable energy for power produces far less greenhouse gases and pollution than fossil fuels, so they are less harmful to our planet.

In this solar power station in Hemau, Bayern, Germany, hundreds of panels capture solar energy and turn it into electricity.

Why discuss solar power?

People have used the Sun's energy, or solar power, for thousands of years for warmth and light, but today we can also use it to make electricity. Globally less than 1 per cent of all electricity comes from solar power. This book explores the advantages and disadvantages of using solar power to meet our growing demand for electricity now and into the future.

How we use the Sun's energy

The Sun is millions of kilometres away from Earth, but it is still our nearest star. Like other stars, the Sun is an enormous ball of incredibly hot gases. Solar energy from the Sun's gases moves through space to Earth in the form of heat and light **radiation**. We can use the energy in the Sun's radiation in different ways.

Solar heating

The simplest way in which we use the Sun's heat is to warm our homes. By building houses with windows that face the Sun, the glass lets heat radiation in to warm the air that is trapped inside. We can heat water using solar collectors. Solar collectors are large glass panels that go on house roofs. Inside the panels are dark pipes that contain liquid. The pipes absorb heat radiation from the Sun and warm the liquid inside. They carry the hot liquid inside the house to heat tanks of water.

Electricity from the Sun

We can also make electricity using the Sun's energy in two ways. In a thermal solar power station, sunlight is used to boil water making high-pressure steam. The moving steam spins the blades of a **turbine**, which looks a bit like a propeller. A machine called a generator then converts the movement energy, or **kinetic energy**, of the turbine into electrical energy. The second way to make electricity from sunlight is with **solar cells**. These are devices that change sunlight directly into electricity in one step.

Solar collectors absorb heat in sunlight and transfer this energy via liquids to water.

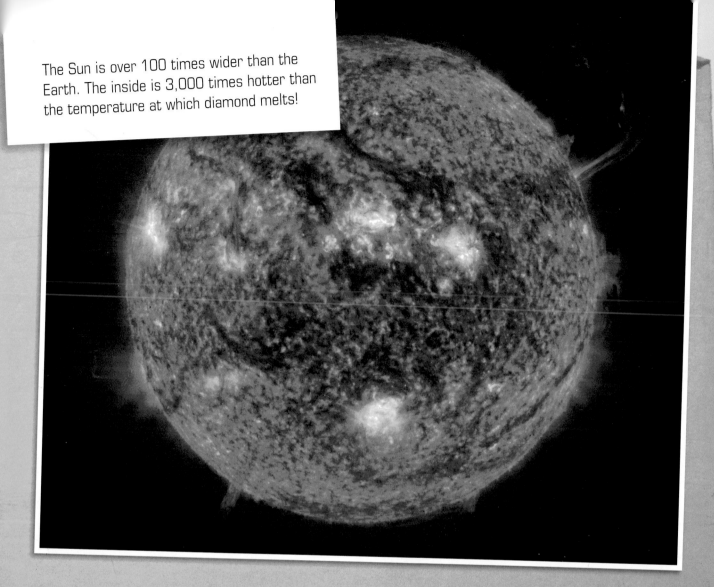

The Sun is over 100 times wider than the Earth. The inside is 3,000 times hotter than the temperature at which diamond melts!

Energy and power

Energy is usually described as the ability to do work. A computer gets the energy it needs to work from electricity. Energy can be measured in units called joules. People often use the word 'power' to mean a supply of electricity. Power is the rate at which energy is used or sent. It is measured in units called watts, which are joules per second. A laptop computer needs 45 watts to make it work. A kilowatt (kW) is 1,000 watts and a megawatt (MW) is 1 million watts.

We can compare how much electricity a home, business or town uses or consumes using units that show the energy used each hour: the kilowatt hour (kWh) or megawatt hour (MWh). People in different countries consume different amounts, depending on how many electrical machines they use. For example, in 2005 an average person in Canada used 17 MWh, whereas an average person in Costa Rica used a tenth of this amount.

Thermal solar power stations

Even on the hottest summer's day, sunlight on a puddle of water only makes it warm. Thermal solar power stations need a way of concentrating solar heat so it can superheat liquids. They use systems of mirrors to reflect, or bounce, sunlight that falls over a large area onto a small area. Then it can be used to make electricity.

Troughs

Some thermal solar plants use mirrors that are shaped like troughs. This shape reflects sunlight that hits any part of the mirror and concentrates it onto a **solar receiver** running along the middle. The receiver is the part that heats up. For a row of troughs the receiver is usually a tube of oil. The oil heats to around 400°C (750°F) and is then pumped to a nearby power block. Here the hot oil flows through tubes in tanks of water. The water boils and the steam is used to generate power.

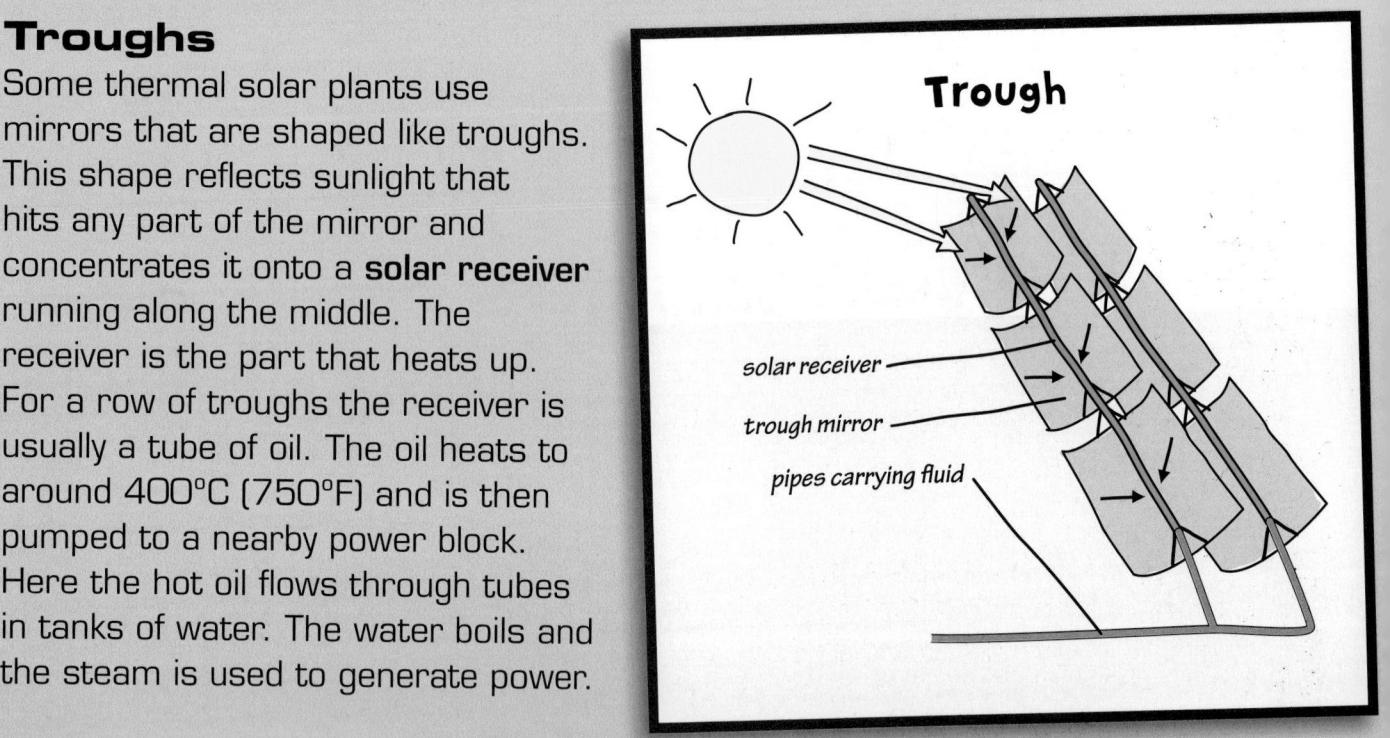

Trough

solar receiver
trough mirror
pipes carrying fluid

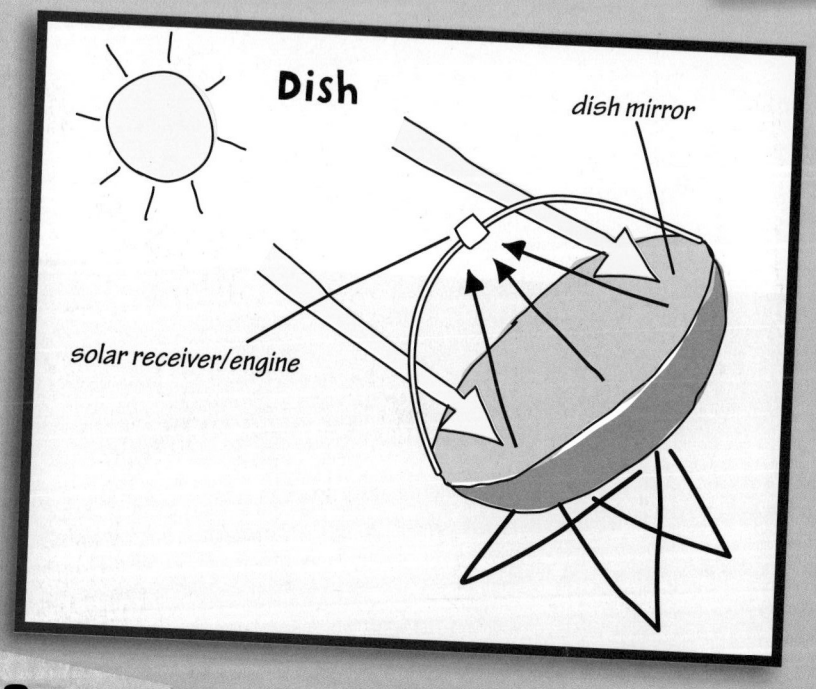

Dish

dish mirror

solar receiver/engine

Dishes

A solar dish works in a similar way but the receiver for each dish-shaped mirror is often a special device called a Stirling engine. When trapped air inside this engine is warmed and expands, it operates a generator.

Solar towers

Other thermal solar plants have a single solar tower surrounded by a number of mirrors. Each mirror is flat and angled so that it reflects sunlight onto a receiver at the top of the tower. Tubes in the receiver contain melted salts which are different from the salt we eat. These salts can get twice as hot as oil and they also stay hot for a long time. The hot salts boil water in the same way as the hot oil, but they contain more heat energy.

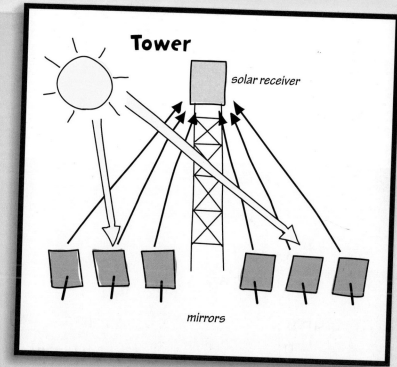

Tower

solar receiver

mirrors

'I am certain that the energy of the future is going to be thermal solar. There is nothing comparable. The sooner we focus on it the better.'

Professor Jack Steinberger, Nobel prize-winning director of the CERN particle physics laboratory in Geneva, 2009

Using rising air

Some power companies have built thermal solar power systems that use rising hot air to make electricity rather than steam. A thermal updraft tower is rather like a very large glass or plastic greenhouse with a tall chimney-shaped tower in the middle. Sunlight warms up the air beneath the glass so it expands and gets lighter. This warm air rises up the tower, spinning turbines in the tower that move generators and generates electricity.

A solar tower receiver in a small thermal solar power station in Israel. Motors underneath the mirrors angle them up or down to direct sunlight.

How solar cells work

A solar cell is a combination of special materials that are sandwiched together in layers. The layers work together to convert light energy from the Sun into electricity. This conversion of energy is called the **photovoltaic** effect. That is why solar cells are also known as photovoltaic or PV cells.

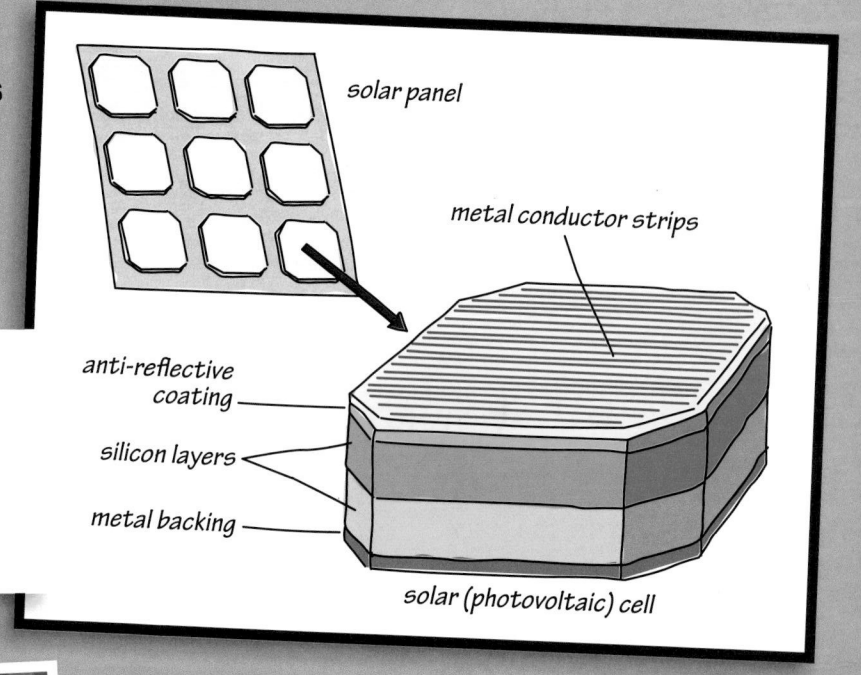

solar panel

metal conductor strips

anti-reflective coating

silicon layers

metal backing

solar (photovoltaic) cell

Solar cells together form solar panels. Glass or plastic on top of the cell protects the silicon inside. It also has a coating to stop useful light reflecting away from the cell.

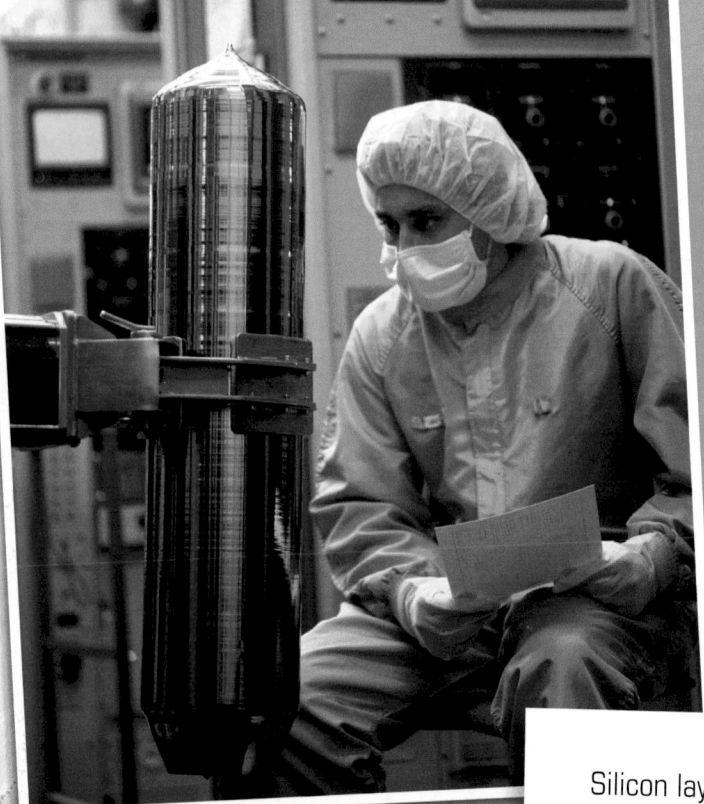

Light energy to electricity

Most solar cells contain two very thin layers of silicon, a material that can be extracted from sand. The silicon in each layer is coated with a different chemical. When light energy hits the silicon layers, it makes a very small electric **current** start to flow between them. Metal strips on top of the cell **conduct** or carry the electricity away from the silicon layers to wires. The wires take the electricity to where it is needed. Individual solar cells are often connected together in **solar panels** to provide more power.

Silicon layers in solar cells are usually thin wafers cut by machine from large silicon crystals made in special factories.

Solar power is a better way to make electricity than fossil fuel power

For:

No fuel or harmful gases

To generate each megawatt of electricity a coal power station burns 2,800 tonnes of coal and releases nearly 6,000 tonnes of carbon dioxide.

Endless massive supply

The Sun will keep burning for millions of years. Enough solar energy hits Earth each second to provide all the world's energy needs for a year.

Against:

No sunlight, no power

Solar cells and thermal solar power stations do not work when the Sun is not shining.

Better than coal

Many modern fossil fuel power stations burn gas, which releases two thirds less carbon dioxide than coal.

Solar power is better than fossil fuel generation as it is renewable and does not cause global warming.

Solar panels are wired together to combine the electricity made by hundreds of connected solar cells.

How solar power varies

Solar power can only be harnessed in the daytime and not at night. But the amount of solar power available also varies day to day, from season to season, and between different places around the world.

Sun and climate

The amount of solar power available to different countries around the world varies greatly depending on climate. Climate is the typical pattern of weather a place has throughout the year. For example, tropical climates are hot and sunny almost all year round. Climates, like those in Europe and most of North America, have generally warm, sunny summers followed by cool, wet winters with fewer hours of sunlight.

Solar power received at Earth's surface

lowest　　　　　　　　　　　highest

The greatest solar power is generally near the Equator and away from the poles. However, this map shows that it varies between different areas of ocean and land.

Solar power availability

Places with sunny, hot climates can create electricity from solar power all year round. The problem for temperate places is that solar power generates more electricity in summer and less in winter. Scientists have not yet found a reliable way to store solar power generated on a sunny summer's day for use in winter. So solar power is not an ideal energy resource for people who need electricity to run heating and lighting systems on cold, dark winter evenings.

Storing solar

Solar power can only be stored for fairly short periods of time. It is mainly stored to be used overnight or to top up other power sources on a cloudy day. One method of storing solar power is as electricity in **batteries**. The problem is that batteries are expensive and lose stored electricity quite quickly. A method used in thermal solar systems is to store solar power as heat. Melted salts are heated in towers and then kept in tanks that prevent them losing heat.

These big towers store molten salt for the Solar Two power station in California, USA.

CASE STUDY

Clouds, global warming and solar power

Many scientists think that global warming is producing fewer clouds close to the Earth that normally reflect sunlight back into space. With fewer clouds there would be more solar power, but also faster global warming. A study by the Copenhagen Consensus Centre in 2009 concluded that we should make clouds to slow global warming. Special sailing ships could suck up seawater and spray it out of tall funnels high into the sky. Water vapour in the atmosphere would collect in clouds around the salty spray. A large fleet of these ships crossing the oceans could make enough cloud to reflect over 1 per cent of sunlight that would otherwise warm the Earth.

Solar cells for different needs

One of the important advantages of solar power is that it can be generated where it is needed. Solar cells can be installed on anything from a calculator to a space station, and from a tent to an office block. This kind of **microgeneration** allows families, small communities and businesses to generate enough electricity for their own needs.

Many satellites and other structures in space get their electricity from solar panels. The International Space Station has solar panels the size of football pitches to power all of its technology!

Remote places

Around 1.5 billion people around the world do not have **mains electricity**. This is mostly because they live in remote places that are not connected to a **grid**, which is the network of cables linking places to power stations in many countries. Solar panels are being introduced in many remote places in sunny countries across the world, from African villages to isolated farms in central Australia. It is far cheaper to supply panels than install cables and in some less developed countries charities may help pay for the panels. Solar radios, computers, lights, pumps and road signs are some of the many microgenerating devices that have a massive impact in remote places.

Built-in power

In microgeneration, solar panels are erected close to or on the structures that will use the electricity they produce. Solar panels are often fixed to roofs of buildings or on the ground near a building. That way there is no need for long cables to take the electricity to the people who use it. Solar panels are often angled so they face the Sun. Being angled also means rain and any dirt run off their surface. Modern buildings sometimes use special solar building materials instead of panels. These include roof tiles and window glass with built-in solar cells.

CASE STUDY

Barefoot College

Barefoot College, in the Indian state of Rajasthan, is helping poor, remote villages in India to use solar power. Villagers attend the college and are trained to be engineers. They learn how to set up and maintain solar cells. These engineers then take solar panels and electric lanterns, many made in the college using local materials, back to their villages. There are now over 400 engineers and they have introduced solar lighting to 12,000 homes and around 1,200 education centres. In the past many children used to miss out on education because they spent their days tending to family cattle. Now they can carry on with family duties and study useful skills such as maths and reading at night schools that are lit up by solar lanterns.

Barefoot College employs local people with local knowledge to distribute, help set up and educate villagers about solar power.

Solar power stations

Solar power stations, which are often called **solar farms**, consist of many solar panels or lots of mirrors linked together. A solar farm generates lots of electricity from one site. A grid takes the electricity from the solar power station to businesses, homes and towns away from the site.

Where to build a solar farm

A solar farm needs a large area of land for two reasons. First, there need to be enough mirrors or panels to harvest a large amount of solar radiation. Secondly, the mirrors and panels need to be spaced out so they do not shade each other. Power companies often build solar farms on wasteland, dry scrubland or deserts. These types of land are usually cheap to buy and the land is fairly level.

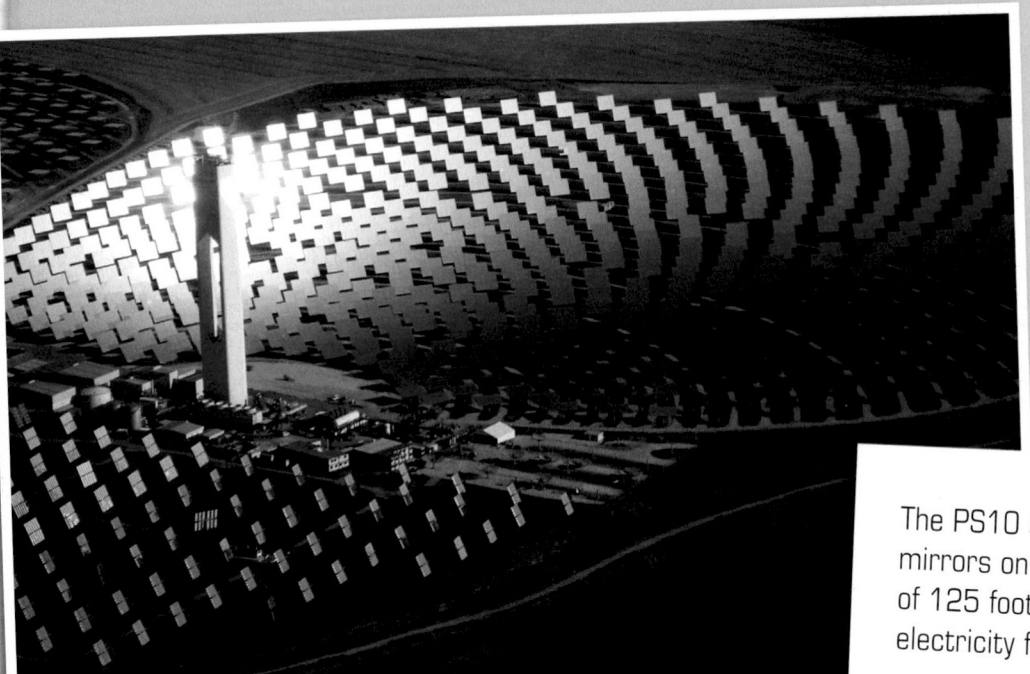

The PS10 solar farm in Spain, has 600 mirrors on 250 hectares – the size of 125 football pitches – to generate electricity for 5,000 local homes.

Power companies usually bulldoze land to remove plants that might get in the way or shade mirrors or panels, and to make sure it is completely flat. Thermal solar plants need level ground so all of the mirrors can reflect lots of light whatever the position of the Sun. An ideal site for thermal solar power stations also has a good water supply nearby, such as a river, to take water for making steam used to turn the turbines.

Are solar farms a good use of space?

No:

Less power
A solar farm that generates 20MW of electricity takes up the same space as a coal power station that makes five times more electricity.

Changing places
Flattening land damages soil and natural **habitats**. Solar power stations use water that local plants and animals need.

Yes:

Lower impact
Solar farms need no fuel to generate electricity. The land impacts of coal power stations include the huge areas miners dig up to find coal.

Using unwanted land
Solar farms are usually built on poor-quality land that is unsuitable for people to live on or farm.

Solar farms are an efficient way to use waste land, so long as power companies try to protect vulnerable habitats.

CASE STUDY

A new farm in the Mojave Desert

A giant solar farm with 20,000 mirror dishes is being built in the Mojave Desert, California, USA. It will generate up to 500 MW of electricity. However, many scientists say that clearing land here damages habitats where rare plants and animals such as the desert tortoise live. The power company says they are taking steps to treat the land carefully and the farm will only use a small amount of water from the area because they use Stirling engines (see page 8).

17

Solar power and pollution

When solar power stations are up and running and generating electricity, they do not produce any gases that are harmful to the atmosphere. However, making solar cells and building solar power stations does cause some pollution. This has impacts on both the atmosphere and on living things.

Releasing greenhouse gases

How does solar power create greenhouse gases? Solar cells are mostly made from silicon. To make silicon, factories burn coal to heat sand and turn it into silicon crystals. Burning coal releases carbon dioxide gas into the atmosphere. Making mirrors, solar towers and the concrete needed to build thermal solar power stations also uses electricity. This mostly comes from fossil fuel power stations that release greenhouse gases. The lorries and other vehicles used to carry solar power parts and clear land for power stations burn diesel oil that also releases greenhouse gases.

This is a view inside a furnace showing red-hot silicon. Lots of energy from burning fuels is needed to melt silicon so it can be shaped into crystals.

Solar cell pollution

Different stages of solar cell production cause other kinds of pollution, too. Small amounts of poisonous substances are used in solar cells. Lead is used in the electrical parts of cells and panels and cadmium is used instead of silicon in some cells. Both of these substances are only poisonous in large quantities. This becomes an issue if they build up in living things over time. A worker in a solar cell factory could breathe in tiny amounts of cadmium or lead when making cells over a long time and gradually become sick.

Let's discuss

Solar power is less polluting than coal power

Against:

Health hazards

Substances used to make solar cells are health hazards, particularly for people who make the cells. Cadmium can cause **cancers** and weak bones.

Greenhouse gases

Clearing land for solar farms can damage soil and plants that normally soak up some of the carbon dioxide from the atmosphere.

For:

Poisonous fuels

Burning coal in power stations releases 300 times more cadmium into the air than making solar cells.

Less gas

A silicon factory releases about 1.5 tonnes of carbon dioxide to make a tonne of silicon cells. A coal station would release 60 tonnes of carbon dioxide to generate the same amount as the cells.

On balance, solar power is far less polluting than coal power.

Mining rocks to extract metals such as lead used in solar cells produces holes and lots of waste rock. Rain can wash away remaining metals from the rock, poisoning rivers and lakes.

How efficient is solar power?

When we switch on an electric light, some electrical energy turns into light and some is wasted as it turns into heat. Like any other power technology, solar power wastes energy, too. Its **efficiency** – how much it wastes – depends on many things.

Comparing efficiency

At present most solar cells are made from silicon, which converts about one-fifth of the solar radiation reaching its surface into electricity. The other four-fifths is wasted. Some solar cells are made from different photovoltaic materials that waste only half of the energy they capture. Thermal solar power stations convert about a third of solar energy hitting their mirrors into electricity, which is as efficient as the conversion of coal into electricity in power stations. However, coal supplies are limited, whereas there is an endless supply of sunlight so wastage is not expensive. However, if solar power stations were more efficient they could make more electricity.

Cables heat up because the metal they are made from slows the flow of current, so some electrical energy converts into heat.

Losing energy

Not all the electricity made in a power station reaches homes and businesses. About 7 per cent of all electricity generated in power stations is lost as heat that escapes from cables as electricity travels through the grid. In general, longer cables lose more electricity than shorter cables. Solar farms are often built on land far from where people live, so they lose more electricity than power stations built nearer to cities.

Heat effect

Solar cells do not use the heat in sunlight to make electricity. When the silicon layers get too hot, the heat can cause problems for solar cells because it stops the electric current from moving into the wires. This is a major reason why solar farms in deserts usually use mirrors. The hotter conditions help warm the solar receiver faster. Solar panel farms are better at generating electricity in bright, cool conditions, for example in parts of Europe, North America and Japan.

Looking after solar farms

Solar cells and mirrors generate less when they are shaded or dirty. As solar panels are made of lots of small cells connected together, when light is blocked from just a few cells they can prevent the whole panel from working. Power company workers look after solar farms by cutting down plants that may shade panels and by checking that the motors to make the mirrors move and to pump melted salt or oil through the pipes work properly. They may also clean the mirrors and cells.

A technician checks a mirror trough installation for any damage, dirt or other problems that might affect its solar efficiency.

The cost of solar power

The major cost of solar power for electricity is building the power stations or making and installing solar panels. Once this is done, the costs for running and looking after a solar power station are low. What's more, there is no fuel to buy as there is for fossil fuel power generation.

Paying for power

All power stations cost a lot to set up before they can start generating electricity. Power companies have to buy land and equipment such as turbines. At present it costs three times more to set up a solar plant than it costs to set up fossil fuel power stations.

Solar power stations cost more to set-up partly because they use newer and more expensive technology. Silicon crystals used to make solar cells are very expensive. At present there are not many factories making silicon, but there are many companies wanting to buy silicon. It is used to make computer and mobile phone parts, as well as solar panels. This means that silicon makers can charge a high price for their sought-after product. One reason why set-up costs for solar power should get cheaper in future is that more solar panels will be made without silicon.

The costs of all the stages in silicon production, from the worker producing silicon crystals in a furnace to finished solar cells, all contribute to the final cost of solar power.

Let's discuss

Is solar power too expensive?

There are good environmental reasons for using solar power, but is the cost of solar power too high for most **consumers**?

Yes:

Comparing costs
Electricity from thermal solar power stations is five times more expensive than electricity from fossil fuel or nuclear power stations. Electricity from solar cells and panels is even more costly.

Expensive renewable
Solar is more expensive than every other kind of renewable energy resource apart from wave power, which uses new technology to capture ocean energy.

No:

Unfair comparisons
The cost of fossil fuel power does not include the effects of global warming. For example, governments give money to farmers whose crops have failed because of extreme weather.

Getting cheaper
Solar power is getting cheaper all the time. Scientists are inventing more efficient and cheaper solar technology that will reduce costs.

The cost of solar power will get closer to other renewables and non-renewables as the cost of solar technology falls.

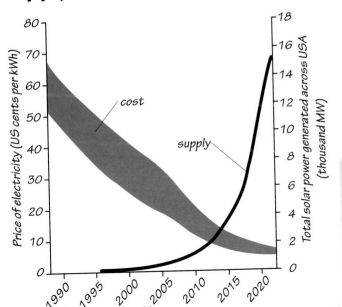

Supply and cost of solar power

The black line shows the possible increase in solar power into the future and the grey line shows how the price of electricity from solar power will probably fall.

Encouraging solar power use

In an attempt to tackle global warming, representatives from governments around the world have met and agreed targets to reduce greenhouse gases released by their countries. To help them achieve these targets, many governments are encouraging solar power industries.

Helping to set up solar power

Governments can **subsidize** new solar projects to help set them up. They make payments or loans to help power companies and individuals pay for the costs of solar technology and installation. Governments may also ask fossil fuel power companies to reduce the greenhouse gases they create. Some power companies that previously relied only on fossil fuels have begun setting up solar farms or other renewable power stations that link in to their mains electricity grid to help them achieve this.

These climate protestors are asking the Canadian government to cut greenhouse gases. Slowing global warming will help protect the habitats where polar bears live.

Buying excess solar electricity

Another way governments encourage solar power is to buy electricity that solar plants or panels generate. When solar power stations or solar panels make more electricity than they need, companies and individuals may feed the extra power into the grid to become mains electricity. It is easier to sell the spare electricity than store it for long periods in batteries. By paying for this renewable electricity, governments encourage companies and individuals to generate more.

CASE STUDY

Solar boom in Germany

In 2000 the German government decided to actively encourage solar power. It made a law to force power companies to pay more for electricity made using solar power than the price they normally sell fossil fuel electricity for. This caused a solar boom in Germany. Farmers put up solar panels in fields, individuals and businesses put panels on their roofs, and new solar companies were founded. By 2009, Germany had over half of the world's solar installations.

Let's discuss

Solar power should be subsidized

Yes:

Encouraging renewables
Encouraging renewables is not only cleaner but also fair because many governments have subsidized non-renewables such as fossil fuel power in the past.

Self-sufficient
Using renewable power such as solar reduces a government's reliance on countries where fossil fuels are found.

No:

The wrong choice
If solar power is suitable to meet global power needs, then it shouldn't need subsidizing. It should survive on its own merits.

Hiding the true cost
Subsidies come from money that people in a country pay their governments. Some people would prefer to choose which power technology to support.

It is a good idea for countries to subsidize solar in order to help develop an independent, clean, renewable power supply.

New solar technology

Solar power technology is quite new. The first solar cells that really worked appeared in the 1950s and thermal solar plants have only been around since the late 1980s. Here are some of the new solar technologies that are being developed today for future use.

Artificial trees

Green leaves can use sunlight to make food for trees even when they are completely shaded. Scientists at Solar Botanic Energy Systems are trying to copy how all the leaves on a tree work together to turn sunlight into power. They plan to design 20 different types of artificial trees with different shapes and designs. The trees will have not only built-in solar cells but also technology to convert heat and the movement of leaves in the wind to make even more electricity!

The Solar Tree invented by Ross Lovegrove has solar panels built into the leaves that generate electricity by day to light the streets at night.

Reshaping solar power

The Cool Earth Solar company has invented a way to make solar power using balloons rather than flat solar panels. Their balloons are 2.5-metres wide, and rounded with clear tops. The curved top of a balloon, made from plastic, focuses sunlight onto the dark, reflective bottom. The light bounces off this towards a solar cell receiver at the top. The company says that their solar cell generates up to 400 times more electricity than other solar cells, for its size, because of the focusing effect of light in the balloon.

Solar power in space

Scientists are hoping to use vast satellites in space in future to beam electricity from solar panels to Earth. In space, solar radiation is more powerful than at the Earth's surface as it has not had to travel through clouds and dust in the Earth's atmosphere. Also, building in space means there are fewer mirrors and panels covering the Earth's surface. It would not be possible to stretch cables from space to Earth, so scientists plan to send the electrical energy as a beam of microwave radiation about 1 km across. It remains to be seen whether power companies and governments are prepared to pay for this expensive technology and also whether it will actually work.

'We'll invest in the development and deployment of solar technology wherever it can thrive and we'll find the best ways to integrate solar power into our electric grid.'

US President Barack Obama, 2009

The Cool Earth Solar balloons can be constructed more cheaply and quickly than normal solar panels.

CASE STUDY   Printing solar cells

The Nanosolar company, set up in 2002, makes solar cells without silicon by printing a special photovoltaic ink onto thin, flexible metal sheets. When sunlight shines on the ink, a current moves through the metal foil and the foil conducts the electricity to wires. Machines can print tens of metres of these 'PowerSheets' each minute, and they cost about one-tenth the price of normal silicon cells for every watt they generate. Printed cells could be on all kinds of surfaces in future, from car roofs to mobile phones.

The future for solar power

The cost of producing energy from renewables is falling and will continue to fall as more countries and individuals look to alternatives to fossil fuels. Meanwhile the cost of fossil fuel power will rise. Because of this solar power will undoubtedly be a growing part of the energy mix in future. Globally, some scientists believe that by 2050 solar power stations could produce up to one quarter of the world's electricity.

Increasing availability

In future, a combination of new technologies and more government commitment to renewable energy resources could bring a big increase in the use of solar power. As more countries invest in solar power and solar technology gets cheaper, more people will be able to afford solar electricity. Better methods for storing thermal solar heat and distributing solar generated power will help these technologies meet demand. More efficient and adaptable solar panels may even be able to generate electricity to power more vehicles and cut use of oil for fuel. Many people believe that it is simpler and cheaper to reduce how much electricity we use than switch to solar. We can all do this in many ways, from turning off lights when we leave a room to buying energy-efficient machines.

Bertrand Piccard invented the Solar Impulse aeroplane in 2009. Its 63-metre wingspan is covered with over 11,000 solar cells powering flight propellers.

Looking ahead

Some regions of the world will expand their use of solar power faster than others. These are generally regions where there is plentiful sunlight, although governments may have different reasons for going solar. In some, such as North Africa, wind or running water are not so plentiful so solar power may be the only renewable energy resource available. In others, such as the USA, solar power will help reduce greenhouse gases and make the country less reliable on fuel from other countries.

Big businesses such as Walmart are installing solar panels on the roofs of some of their stores, such as this one in Palm Desert, California, as solar power grows in global popularity.

CASE STUDY

The future lies in the desert

In future, solar power could become more widely available if it can be transported from deserts where the sun is very strong and there are few clouds, to cooler temperate regions where the usage of electricity is high. There are plans to build a solar power network in the Sahara covering a total area the size of Wales, UK. One of the biggest challenges is building new long-distance power transmission lines that do not lose much electricity. If the scheme works, experts believe that the countries of North Africa could supply enough electricity for almost the whole of Europe!

Solar activity

Create a solar cooker

You can make a very simple solar trough that collects enough sunlight to cook with. It works rather like the thermal solar troughs on page 8.

What you need:
- Shoebox without lid
- Thin card such as half an office folder
- Tape
- Aluminium cooking foil
- Ruler
- Bamboo barbeque skewer longer than the box
- Marshmallows

1 Drape the card over the box so it hangs down in a half pipe shape and tape in place.

2 Smooth the foil over the card and tape down the edges.

3 Measure half the depth from the top of the box to the bottom of the trough and draw a line at this level on the outside end of the box. **CAREFULLY** push the skewer through the box on this line, exactly half way across the box end. Thread on marshmallows before pushing the skewer out the other end.

4 Put the box outside on a sunny day and angle it towards the Sun. The shape of the trough will reflect sunlight onto the marshmallows and melt them!

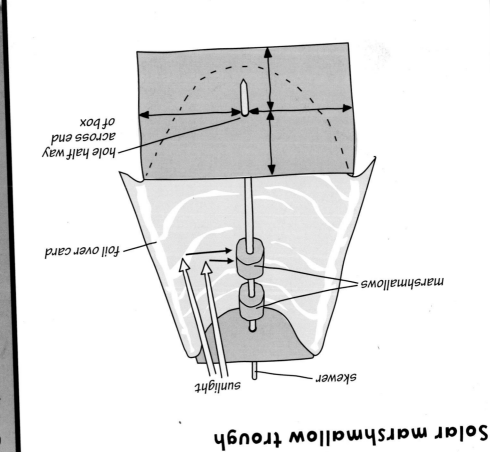

Solar marshmallow trough

hole half way across end of box

foil over card

marshmallows

sunlight

skewer

Solar topics and glossary

History

- People were using technology such as magnifying glasses and mirrors to heat things using the Sun's radiation in ancient Greek and Roman times. Make a timeline of how people have used solar power since then.

Geography

- Many different factors affect how hot or sunny a place is apart from its position on the Earth. Research altitude, albedo effect and smog.

Design and Technology

- What features would a solar-powered car or aeroplane need? Design your own solar-powered vehicle. For some inspiration find out about the Solar Challenge car race and the recent Solar Impulse aeroplane (see picture on page 28).

English

- Write an imaginary diary from the year 2200 describing life without coal, gas and oil, but with widespread renewable power.

Science

- Find out about the effects of global warming on the following ecosystems: Arctic sea ice, coral reefs.

Glossary

atmosphere mix of gases surrounding the Earth up to the edge of space.

battery store of electrical energy.

cancer disease in which abnormal cells grow and kill normal body cells.

carbon dioxide gas found in air that is produced by living things, or by burning fossil fuels.

conduct allow electricity to pass through. Copper in electric wires conducts well.

consumer person who buys services or products such as electricity or cars.

current flow of electricity.

efficiency when resources, such as energy, are made best use of and are not wasted.

fossil fuel fuel such as coal formed over millions of years from remains of living things.

global warming increase in the average temperature of the Earth's atmosphere and oceans.

greenhouse gas gas such as carbon dioxide that stores heat in the atmosphere.

grid system of wires and pylons for sending electricity across a wide area.

habitat place where particular types of animals or plants normally live.

kinetic energy energy produced by movement.

mains electricity electricity supplied through the grid to users from power stations.

microgeneration small-scale production of electricity to meet the needs of users.

non-renewable energy resource such as coal that is running out as it is not replaced when used.

photovoltaic with the property of converting sunlight into electricity.

pollution harmful substances that make air, water or soil less safe to use or live in.

power station factory for generating electricity.

radiation energy that moves in narrow lines or rays.

renewable energy resource that is replaced naturally and can be used without running out.

solar cell device usually containing silicon that converts solar to electrical energy.

solar farm area with many solar thermal mirrors or solar panels to generate electricity.

solar panel structure containing solar cells linked together to increase electricity output.

solar receiver part of solar thermal system that mirrors focus heat upon.

subsidize pay to support something and encourage its success.

turbine machine for converting linear into mechanical kinetic energy.

Find out more and index

Find out more

Websites

www.eia.doe.gov/kids/energyfacts/
sources/renewable/solar
  Learn more about solar power, renewable
  and non-renewable energy

www1.eere.energy.gov/kids/roofus/
  Check out how we can use solar power
  at home to be energy efficient

Books

*The Environment Detective Investigates:
Saving Energy* by Jen Green (Wayland,
2010)

Solar Power (Energy Sources) by Neil
Morris (Franklin Watts, 2007)

Solar Power (Looking at Energy) by Fiona
Reynoldson (Wayland, 2005)

Index

The Body

Muscles

Veronica Ross

Chrysalis Children's Books

First published in the UK in 2004 by
Chrysalis Children's Books
An imprint of Chrysalis Books Group PLC
The Chrysalis Building, Bramley Road, London W10 6SP

ISBN 1 84138 094 6

British Library Cataloguing in Publication Data
for this book is available from the British Library.

Editorial manager: Joyce Bentley
Editors: Rosalind Beckman, Joe Fullman
Illustrator: Chris Forsey
Designer: Wladek Szechter
Picture researcher: Jenny Barlow

Printed in China

10 9 8 7 6 5 4 3 2 1

Words in **bold** can be found in Words to remember on page 30.

Picture credits
Angela Hampton/Family Life Picture Library: 10, 12, 13, 14, 17.
Chrysalis Images/Ray Moller: 7, 18, 20.
Corbis: LWA-Dann Tardif Front Cover (Main), 4,5; Norbert Schaefer FC (Inset) , 1, 6; Jose Luis
Pelaez, Inc. FC (Inset), 9T; Larry Williams FC (Inset), 26; Gerhard Steiner FC (Inset), 24; Jim
Erickson 15; Franco Vogt 16; Darwin Wiggett 19; Strauss/Curtis 27.
Digital Vision: 9B.
Getty Images: Nick Clements 23.
ImageState: 21.
Stockbyte: 25.
Illustrations: Chris Forsey 8, 11, 22, 28, 29, back cover (inset).

Contents

Look at me!

I can jump. I can dance. I can **blink** and smile. **Muscles** all over my body help me to move and do all the things I want to do.

You use your muscles every time you move. Without them you could not run, walk or jump.

Strong muscles
in your legs help
you to hop when
you play hopscotch.

Where are my muscles?

There are **muscles** all over your body. You have muscles in your face, head, tongue, neck, shoulders, chest, tummy, bottom, legs, arms and hands. There are more muscles in your body than **bones**.

Stick out your tongue and wiggle it around. Your tongue is one of the most powerful muscles in your body.

You have more than 670 muscles in your body.

Do you **shrug** your shoulders if you don't know the answer to a question? The muscles in your shoulders help you do this.

What are muscles?

Muscles are the tough, stretchy parts in your body that help you to move. They come in different shapes and sizes because they do different jobs.

This drawing shows the long muscles in your legs.

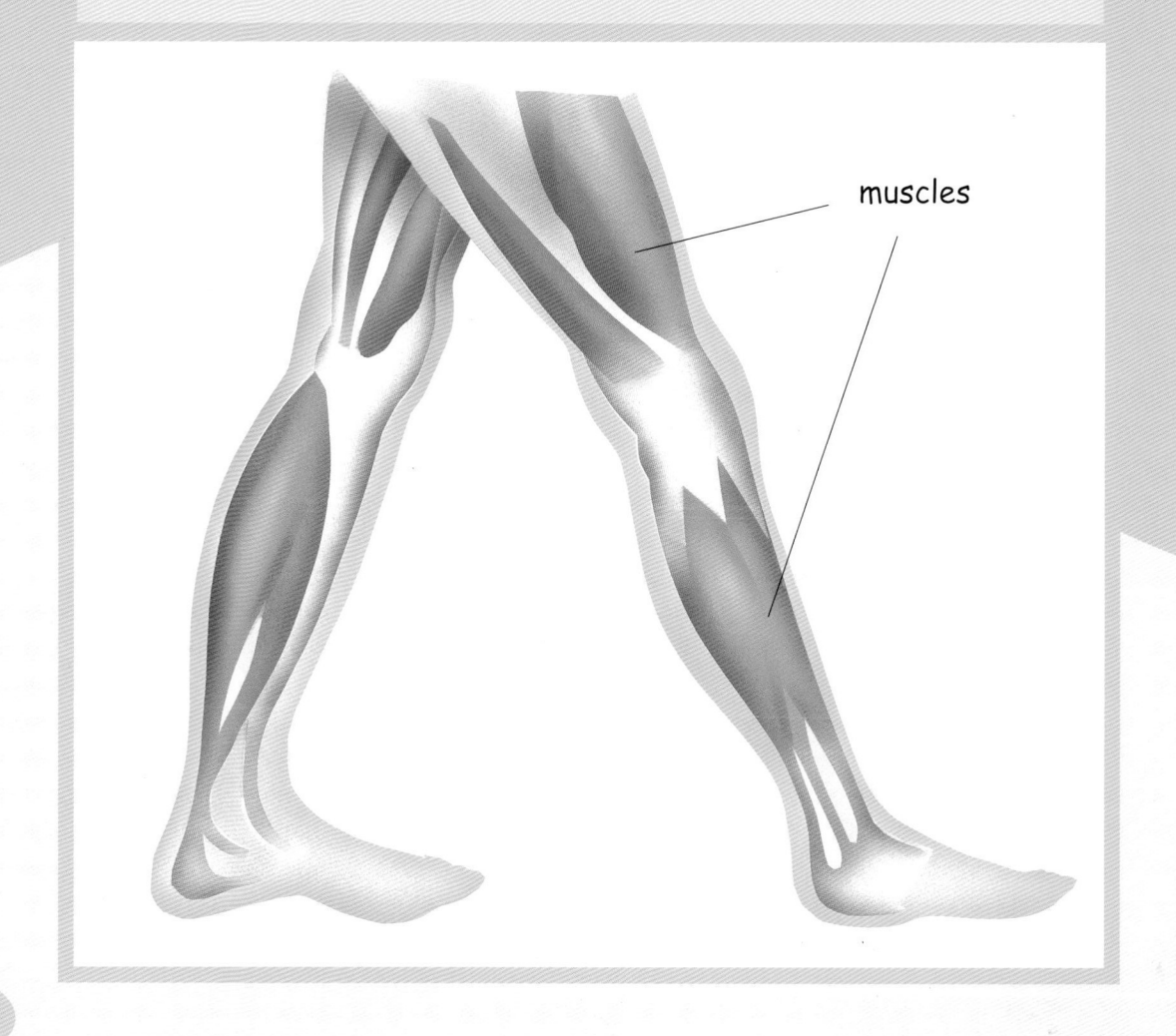

muscles

Some of the biggest muscles are in your back. These muscles help you bend or lift a heavy pile of books.

Small muscles around your eyes let you look up and down, and from side to side.

How do muscles work?

Many muscles work in pairs. They pull on the bones that form your **skeleton** and make them move.

You can see your muscles pushing up under your skin if you bend your arm and make a fist.

All your muscles are **controlled** by your **brain**. It sends out messages to tell the muscles what to do.

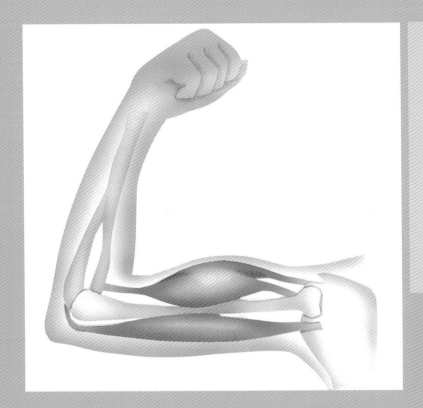

When you bend your arm, the muscle at the top of your arm gets thicker and shorter. It pulls on the bone in the front of your arm to pull your arm up.

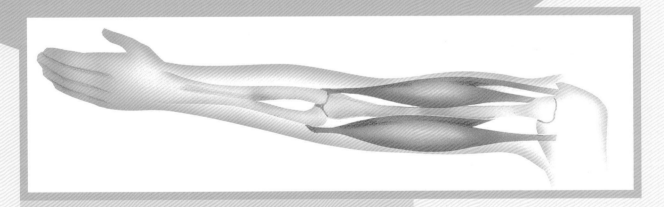

The muscle at the back of your arm pulls your arm down again.

Tummy muscles

The food that you swallow passes down a tube into your stomach. Strong muscles in your stomach walls help to turn the food over and squeeze it until it is soft and mushy.

Your stomach muscles help you to bend forward.

Your tummy muscles
help you to bend over and touch
your toes, and twist around.

When you are sick, the tummy muscles
push the food back out of your stomach,
up your throat and out of your mouth. Yuk!

Arms and hands

Large, strong muscles in your arms give you strength to pick up things.

When you play the piano, your brain sends messages to your hand and wrist muscles to help them move your hands quickly across the keys.

Small muscles in your hands and wrists
help you to make **delicate** movements,
such as holding a pencil and writing a letter.

Hands and wrists
move in lots of ways. You
can grip a book or gently
turn the pages.

Leg work

The muscles in your legs need to be strong, because they help to carry the weight of your body when you stand up and when you walk around.

Your leg muscles give you the power to jump high in the air.

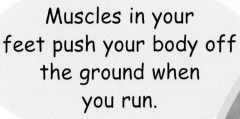

Muscles in your feet push your body off the ground when you run.

Your muscles are very heavy. They make up half your body's weight.

Funny faces

There are lots of tiny muscles in your face. You use these muscles when you smile, **frown**, shout and cry, or when you make silly faces.

When you are suprised, muscles open your mouth wide and raise your eyebrows.

When you smile you use about 20 muscles, but when you frown you use about 40 muscles.
So it's easier to smile!

Look in a mirror and see how many different funny faces you can make.

On your bottom

Two big, rounded muscles cover the bony part of your bottom. When you sit down, the muscles make a soft, squashy cushion.

Sitting on the bony part of your bottom would be painful. Your bottom muscles pad the bone and make sitting much more comfortable.

When you stand up, the muscles tighten
to pull your bottom upwards and forwards.

The muscles
in your bottom also
help to keep your
back straight.

Heartbeat

Your **heart** is a special type of muscle. It pumps **blood** around your body and **beats** all day and all night.

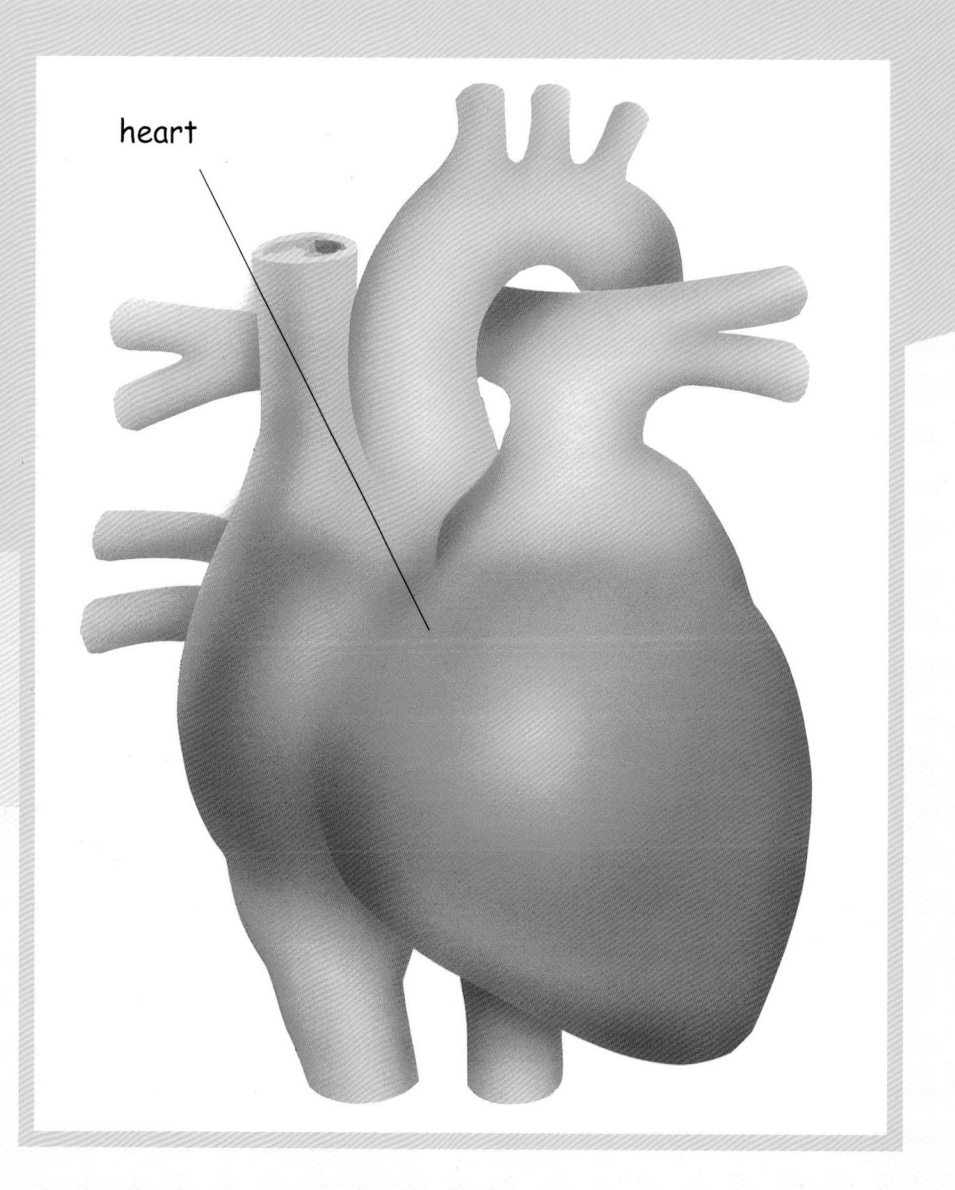

heart

Your heart is inside your chest.

The blood supplies your body with the **oxygen** it needs to make **energy**. Your heart works very hard, so it is a very strong muscle.

You can feel your heart beating if you have been running.

Feeding your muscles

Your muscles do a great job, but to keep them working properly you need to look after them. A good way to do this is to eat healthy food.

A breakfast of cereal, fruit and a glass of milk is a good way to start the day.

Foods such as fruit and vegetables, beans, fish and chicken will keep your muscles in good working order.

Body-building foods such as milk, cheese, nuts and cereals are good for building muscles.

Exercise

Exercise is the best way to look after your muscles. It keeps them strong and **supple**.

Swimming makes the muscles in your legs and arms stronger.

Dancing, gymnastics or just playing chase in the park are really good ways to exercise and to keep fit and healthy.

Before you exercise, do some stretching and bending to warm up. If your muscles are warm they will work better.

Sometimes muscles **tear**. This can happen if you fall or exercise too hard. A good rest will help the muscle heal.

Muscles at work

Now that you know where some of your muscles are, try these exercises and see if you can feel the muscles working.

Bend your leg as if you were about to kick a ball. Can you feel the muscles at the back of your leg tighten? Now kick the ball and feel the muscles at the back of your leg **relax**.

Try moving
your head up and down
to feel the muscles
in your neck.

Words to remember

beat To pump. When your heart beats, it pumps blood around your body.

blink To close your eyes for a second.

bones The hard, tough parts inside your body that make up your skeleton.

blood The red liquid full of oxygen that is pumped around your body by your heart.

brain The soft part inside your head that controls everything you think and do.

control To be in charge of things that happen.

delicate Something that is very precious and needs to be looked after carefully. Delicate movements are careful and gentle.

energy The power you need to be able to do all the things you want to do.

frown To look worried or angry.

heart The muscle that pumps blood around your body.

muscles The soft, stretchy parts inside your body that make you move.

oxygen A gas found in the air that need in order to breathe.

relax To make your muscles looser.

shrug To raise your shoulders. You might shrug if you don't know the answer to a question.

skeleton All the bones in your body.

stomach A large muscle in your body where food is stored before it is broken down to be digested by your body.

supple Moving or bending easily.

tear To rip and come apart.

Index

SYLVIA'S BOOKSHOP

The Story of Paris's Beloved Bookstore and Its Founder (As Told by the Bookstore Itself!)

Robert Burleigh   Illustrated by Katy Wu

A PAULA WISEMAN BOOK

Simon & Schuster Books for Young Readers

New York   London   Toronto   Sydney   New Delhi

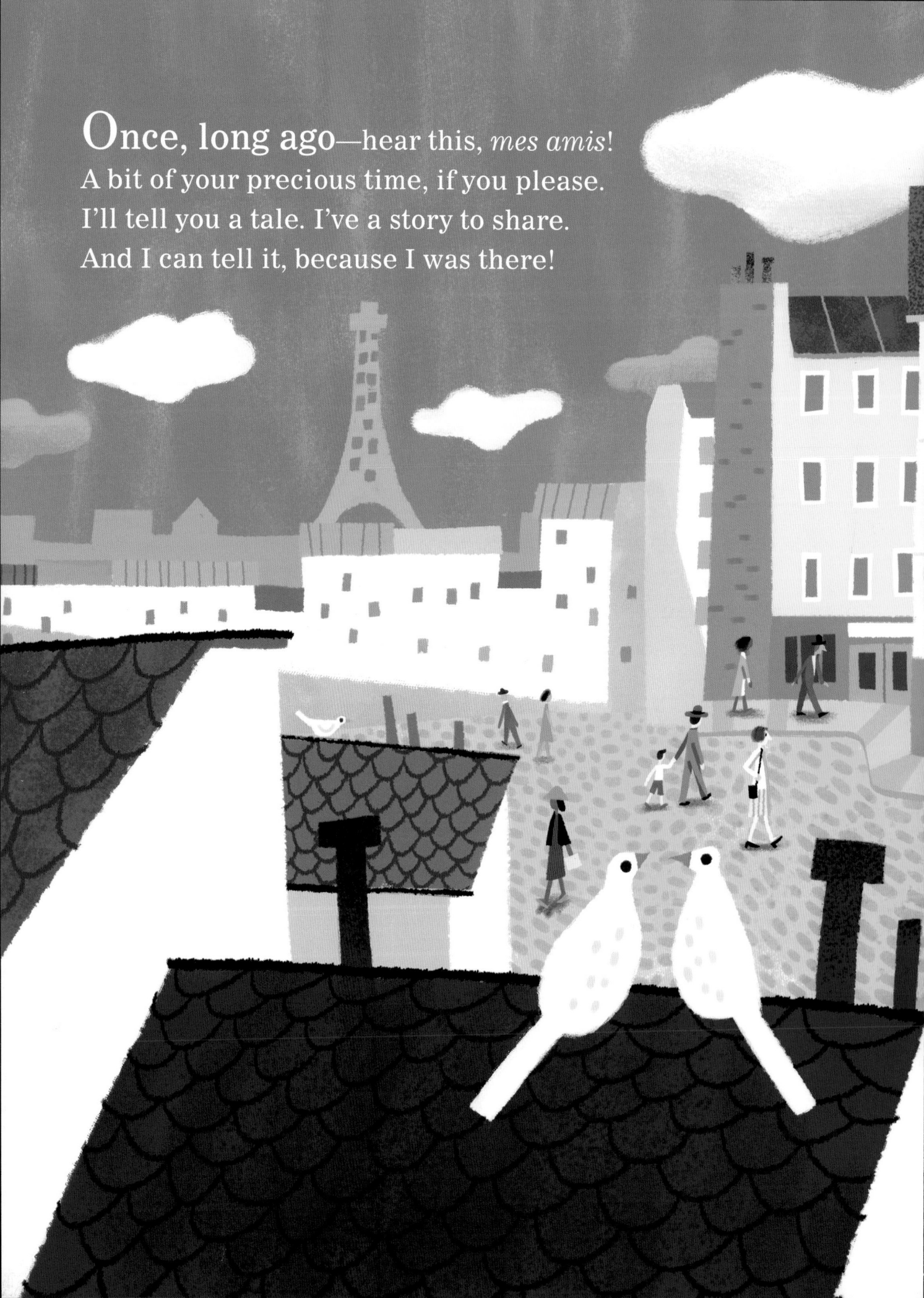

Once, long ago—hear this, *mes amis*!
A bit of your precious time, if you please.
I'll tell you a tale. I've a story to share.
And I can tell it, because I was there!

A bookshop can't talk?
Not true! Not true!
Because *I* can, my friends—see, I'm talking to you!
On a small street in Paris, I slept through the years.
I watched from my windows. Laughter and tears.

Then Sylvia came and changed everything.
An American free spirit as fresh as the spring.
A lover of life—and poetry, too—
Who brought dreams to Paris and made them come tr

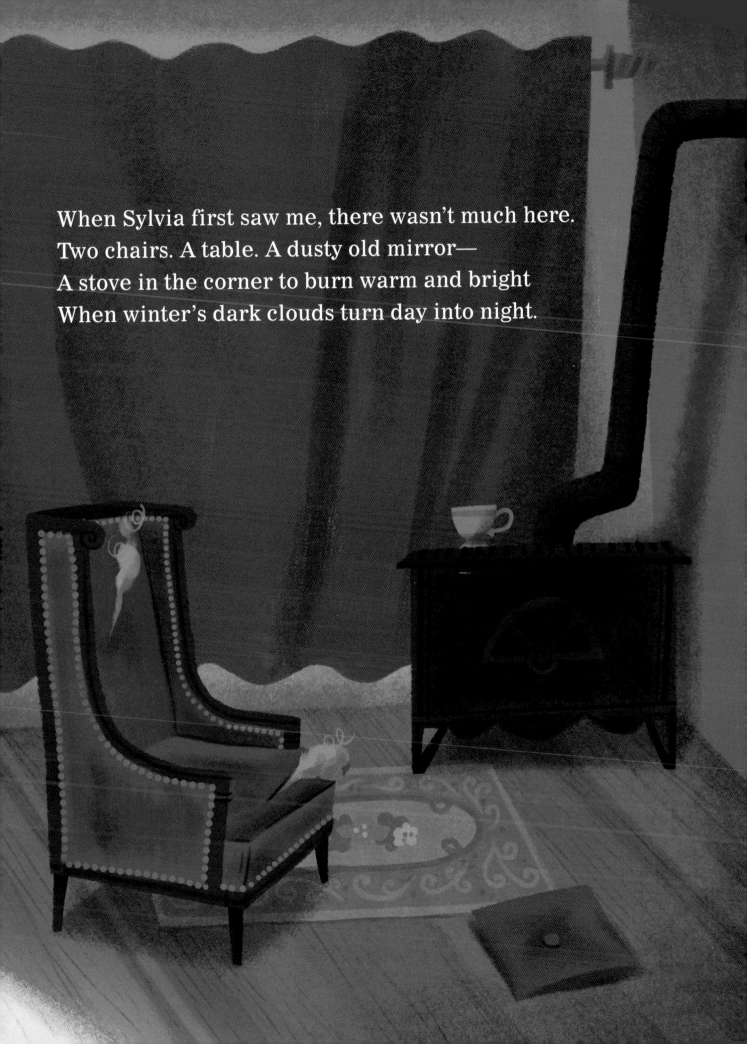

When Sylvia first saw me, there wasn't much here.
Two chairs. A table. A dusty old mirror—
A stove in the corner to burn warm and bright
When winter's dark clouds turn day into night.

Now she flings wide my shutters—sunflowers, blue sky!
The *clip-clop* of horses. A street seller's cry.

"Aha!" Sylvia laughed when she walked in the door.
"What we need here is books, from ceiling to floor!"

On my walls, writers gaze out from times long ago:
Shakespeare, Jane Austen, Walt Whitman, and Poe.
She whispers: "I love it! A magical spot!
Books are my treasures—the best that I've got."

"Books are like rivers that flow through my head.
Books are like roads," she just might have said.

"Roads that connect my old self to my new,
Unlocking our hearts to what's noble and true."

Here's a book like a butterfly perched in your hand.

Here's a book filled with scenes from a faraway land.

Here's a book like a seed that will grow in your mind.

Here's a book that will show you: to seek is to find.

Now sunlight floods in as the Seine flows along.
Each day is a party. Each day is a song.

On a cobblestoned street in the City of Lights,
My door is wide open long into the nights.

Here's Gertrude and Janet. They loudly recite—
From sonnets and ballads. It's a poetry fight!

Scott waltzes around with a book and a smile.
"Listen to this: It's my great 'Gatsby' style!"

James peers through his glasses. He looks like an owl.

Or a monk looking out from under a cowl.

What's never been written!
What's never been read!

What's never been said?

What's lively?

What's fun?

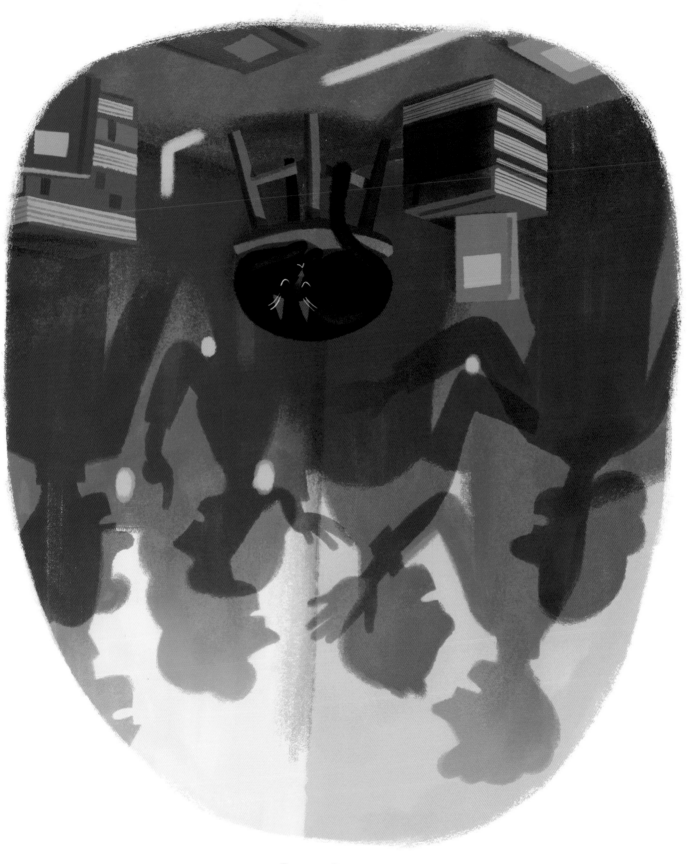

Our black cat (called Lucky) curls into a ball,
And purrs in the corner, in spite of it all.

Sylvia grins. Offers everyone tea.
Introduces her friends to each other—and me.

The lamps come on slowly, just one at a time.
As if they are trying to make up a rhyme.

The party is over. It will start again soon.
Come back tomorrow at more or less noon!

The moonlight beams down into Sylvia's shop.
She dusts, straightens cushions. No time to stop.

Then closes my shutters and hops on her bike,
Saying, "This is the life that I really like."

Yes, once, long ago—my walls were like arms
Around Sylvia's books, and all of their charms.
Just a little old shop, with an old iron key,
But the world I contained was as wide as the sea.

You're near the end, now. This book that you hold
Is whispering "good night," its tale all told.
But maybe, dear friends, we'll meet someday,
In magical Paris, in a time faraway.

SHAKESPEARE AND COMPANY 12

Till then, you can travel through time (and through space)
By opening a book—anywhere, anyplace!

Hurrah for Books and Bookstores!

To hold a book in your hand, to slowly turn the pages, to read, to wonder—there's nothing quite like it. The pages are filled with excitement, with useful or fun information, with new ideas, or with just a means of relaxing for an hour or two, away from the noise of work and the world.

But it hasn't always been this way. In earlier times (say, in Roman times, roughly 2,000 years ago) few people could read and there was no printing. The books that existed then had to be handwritten and mostly kept in a few libraries. Only the privileged could read them.

The invention of printing, however, (around 1450) slowly changed all that. It was now easier to make books, and as more people learned to read, books were soon in greater demand. A new world opened up. Libraries expanded, and bookstores began to flourish.

Over the last few centuries, as bookstores became both places for bookselling and buying—they also became meeting places for people who loved books and ideas that came from books. Writers and readers met, and still meet, to welcome the latest book, to meet new authors, and to discuss (and sometimes argue) about the value of this or that book or magazine. Yes, books are more than words. They contain ideas that matter!

Shakespeare and Company

Sylvia Beach's Shakespeare and Company was such a bookstore. The original Shakespeare and Company that this book tells about opened in Paris in 1919 at 8 rue Dupuytren before moving to a bigger location a few streets over at 12 rue de l'Odéon in 1920. It closed in 1941, around the start of World War II. Here is some information about the people mentioned in this story. They are all real people who often came to Shakespeare and Company.

Sylvia Beach (1887–1962) was a free-spirited American woman who loved books so much that she started a bookshop in Paris, France. (Paris is sometimes called "The City of Lights.") Her bookshop became the meeting place for many important and famous American and French writers who lived in Paris around 100 years ago—shortly after World War I.

And the bookshop? Sylvia named it Shakespeare and Company. Why? She hoped that the writers who visited her shop would be inspired by the spirit of the great English poet and dramatist, William Shakespeare.

Here are a few facts about the writers mentioned in the story:

Who was Ernie?

Ernest Hemingway (1899–1961) was one of the most important American writers of the twentieth century. His stories and novels often dealt with soldiers or people struggling against nature. He received the Nobel Prize in Literature in 1954.

Who was Gertrude?

Gertrude Stein (1874–1946) was an experimental writer of poetry, novels, and plays. She was an American citizen, but lived in France most of her life.

Who was Janet?

Janet Flanner (1892–1978) was the long-time Paris correspondent for *The New Yorker* magazine. Born in the United States, Flanner spent many years in Paris writing about the arts and other subjects. She was a friend of many writers and artists who lived in or visited Paris.

Who was Scott?

F. Scott Fitzgerald (1896–1940) and his wife Zelda (1900–1948) were both writers living at times in Paris during the 1920s. Scott's *The Great Gatsby* is today thought to be one of the foremost American novels.

Who was James?

James Joyce (1882–1941) was an Irish poet and novelist living in Paris. His long novel *Ulysses* is often considered the greatest English-language novel of the twentieth century. Its action takes place in one day in Dublin, Ireland. And guess who helped Joyce publish the first edition of his now-famous book? None other than Sylvia Beach!

Who was Simone?

Simone de Beauvoir (1908–1986) was a French novelist, literary critic, and philosopher. In all her writing, she defended every woman's right to have a fulfilling life.

Who was Man Ray?

Man Ray (1890–1976) was the special name taken by the American-born artist and photographer Emmanuel Radnitzky, who spent much of his adult life working in Paris and was friends with many other well-known artists and writers.

And finally:
Is there still a Shakespeare and Company bookstore in Paris?

Yes, again! Sadly, Sylvia was forced to close her store in 1940 when the German army occupied Paris. (She was later briefly arrested for her anti-Nazi opinions and for helping Jewish friends escape.)

But today another Shakespeare and Company stands proudly in Paris, not in the same location as Sylvia's, but with just as much love of books and literature. Check it out the next time you visit the City of Lights!

Vive la France!
Learn some French, too, and wow your friends!
"Mes amis" (pronounced: mays ah-meez) is French for "my friends."
And "c'est vrai" (pronounced: say vray) means "it's true."

To Sylvia's Bookshop and bookstores around the world.
—R. B.

To my mentor and friend, Mike
—K. W.

SIMON & SCHUSTER BOOKS FOR YOUNG READERS
An imprint of Simon & Schuster Children's Publishing Division
1230 Avenue of the Americas, New York, New York 10020
Text copyright © 2018 by Robert Burleigh
Illustrations copyright © 2018 by Katy Wu
All rights reserved, including the right of reproduction in whole or in part in any form.
SIMON & SCHUSTER BOOKS FOR YOUNG READERS is a trademark of Simon & Schuster, Inc.
For information about special discounts for bulk purchases, please contact Simon & Schuster Special Sales at
1-866-506-1949 or business@simonandschuster.com.
The Simon & Schuster Speakers Bureau can bring authors to your live event. For more information or to book an event,
contact the Simon & Schuster Speakers Bureau at 1-866-248-3049 or visit our website at www.simonspeakers.com.
Book design by Krista Vossen
The text for this book was set in News 705.
The illustrations for this book were rendered digitally.
Manufactured in China
0718 SCP
First Edition
2 4 6 8 10 9 7 5 3 1
CIP data for this book is available from the Library of Congress.
ISBN 978-1-4814-7245-6
ISBN 978-1-4814-7246-3 (eBook)